the little book of Bird Prayers

kevin mayhew

Introduction

Every picture, they say, tells a story, and that was certainly so for me in preparing this book. The photographs captured my imagination the moment I saw them, speaking not just of birds but of life itself: of situations, concerns and needs common to us all. Flip through the pages and you'll readily appreciate what I mean. Bird lover or otherwise, you'll find the images here not only appealing but also evocative, touching a chord deep within. They remind us that we don't have to be 'heavy' to be meaningful. A few words can say as much as many, the ordinary point to things far deeper, and that's as true in prayer as anywhere. We may glimpse God in the 'religious' but can discover him equally in the world around us. For some it's the beauty of a flower that stirs the spirit, for others a scenic view, for others a bustling city . . . for others again, birds – and if that seems strange then read on, for once you've read this little book you'll see both them and God in a new light. These pages offer not simply images to delight in but also a resource for prayer; material, in short, to warm the heart and nurture the spirit.

Nick Fawcett

To my nephew, Dan,
with love and best wishes

When I call to you, Lord, but find no answer,
when I seek for your presence,
but search in vain,
teach me to look more closely
until I find.

I'm sorry, Lord,
for I hoard up worthless trinkets
neglecting what's of real value:
treasure in heaven.
Remind me that all that glistens is not gold.

However small I am,
however insignificant compared to others,
teach me, Lord, that with your help
I can do great things.

Thank you, Lord,
for your mighty hand fashioned the universe,
creating everything that is
and has been and ever shall be,
yet that same hand gently encircles me each day,
enveloping me in love.

Instead of settling, Lord, for a superficial faith,
may I dig deeper,
looking always to discover new delights,
fresh food for my soul.

Teach me, Lord,
that just as you value the humble sparrow,
commonplace though it may be,
so you value everything you have made,
each one of us special in your eyes.

You call me, Lord, to a journey of faith,
venturing out into the unknown.
Help me to respond
to your still small voice within,
and to follow where you lead.

Give me, Lord,
a sense of awe in your presence,
a glimpse of your greatness and grandeur.
Save me from so forgetting
who and what you are
that I stand before you
and fail to marvel.

Thank you, Lord,
for my spirit was chained,
shackled to this world,
but you gave me wings,
and set me free.

Draw me closer, Lord,
to you and those around me,
overcoming whatever keeps us apart
and uniting us in love.

Time and again, Lord, in time of trouble,
you have stretched out your hand
and provided for my needs.
For the constancy of your care,
thank you.

Forgive me, Lord,
for I freeze you out of my life,
faith growing cold within me.
Break the ice that comes between us,
and thaw my frosty heart.

Make my life, Lord, a sign to others,
an emblem of your love,
pointing to your kingdom
and speaking unmistakably of you.

Reach out, Lord, to our broken world –
scarred by hatred,
fractured by division,
ravaged by war –
and, in your mercy, grant us peace.

Thank you, Lord,
for you not only sowed the seed,
but did the spadework too,
preparing the ground in my life,
so that your love could take root
and grow within me.

Help me to live in this world, Lord,
celebrating all it has to offer,
yet still to look to you,
keeping in sight things above.

Keep me focused, Lord,
single-minded in your service.
Help me to fasten my eyes
on you and your kingdom,
and let nothing distract me from that end.

Too easily, Lord, I'm swayed by appearances,
by beauty that's skin-deep.
Teach me, whomever I meet,
to look beyond outward show
to the person underneath.

You call me, Lord, to fish for people,
winning hearts for you,
but too often I leave it to others,
not knowing where to start.
Forgive me,
and, however ill-equipped I feel,
help me to take the plunge.

In a world of hunger, Lord,
where so many find their plate empty,
teach me to appreciate my plenty
and to share it with others.

Give me wisdom to know you, Lord,
intelligence to understand you better,
perception to grasp your will,
and discernment to follow you faithfully.

Pardon my folly, Lord,
for you've created such a beautiful world
and too often it passes me by.
Teach me to make time to stand and stare.

Teach me, Lord,
that I can't sit on the fence for ever,
that your love demands a response –
for or against.
Help me to make up my mind.

Forgive me, Lord,
for I see some things so often
that I lose sight of their beauty,
foolishly dismissing them as ordinary.
Help me to see the unique in the familiar,
the special in the everyday.

Thank you, Lord,
for you have given me life
and called me your child.
Nurture me,
and help me to grow.

I try to hide from you, Lord,
to evade your searching gaze,
but nothing escapes your all-seeing eye.
Teach me, though, that I have nothing to fear,
for you watch over me not to hurt but to help,
not to harm but to heal.

You have put a new song into my mouth, Lord,
a song of joy and thanksgiving,
awe and celebration.
I will make music to you in my heart –
a melody of praise and worship.

Apologies, Lord, for you speak
but I fail to recognise your call.
Help me to listen
and to hear your voice.

Also available:

The Little Book of Mouse Prayers – 1501054
The Little Book of Cat Prayers – 1501055
The Little Book of Dog Prayers – 1501056
The Little Book of Bear Prayers – 1501057
The Little Book of Rabbit Prayers – 1501093
The Little Book of Farm Animal Prayers – 1501094
The Little Book of Wild Animal Prayers – 1501095

First published in 2008 by

KEVIN MAYHEW LTD
Buxhall, Stowmarket, Suffolk, IP14 3BW
E-mail: info@kevinmayhewltd.com
Website: www.kevinmayhew.com

9 8 7 6 5 4 3 2 1 0

ISBN 978 1 84867 016 7
Catalogue No. 1501096

Design by Chris Coe

Images used under licence from Shutterstock, Inc
Image on page 22 © Kerioak/Fotolia.com

Printed and bound in the EU